169

THE GANGES

Written and photographed by

David Cumming

Wayland

THE WORLD'S RIVERS

The Amazon
The Danube
The Ganges
The Mississippi
The Nile
The Rhine
The Seine
The Thames
The Volga
The Yellow River

Cover *Pilgrims gather at one of the main ghats at Varanasi for a ritual bathe in the holy Ganges.*

Series and book editor Rosemary Ashley
Series designer Derek Lee
Book designer Paul Bennett

First published in 1993 by
Wayland (Publishers) Limited
61 Western Road, Hove, East Sussex,
BN3 1JD, England

British Library Cataloguing in Publication Data
David Cumming
Ganges.—(World's Rivers Series)
I. Title II. Series
915.4

ISBN 0-7502-0430-3

Typeset in the UK by
Dorchester Typesetting Group Ltd
Printed in Italy by G. Canale C.S.p.A.
Bound in France by AGM

CONTENTS

1. 'MOTHER GANGES'
4

2. FROM THE MOUNTAINS TO THE SEA
7
The upper Ganges
7
The middle Ganges
9
The lower Ganges
11
The Sundarbans
12

3. WEATHER AND CLIMATE
15
The three seasons
15
The monsoon
15
Cyclones and surges
18

4. AGRICULTURE
20
The effects of weather and terrain
20
The crops
22
Irrigation
23
Social and political problems
24
The Green Revolution in India
26

5. TRANSPORT, CITIES AND INDUSTRIES
28
An important trade route
28
Allahabad
30
Kanpur
30
Varanasi
32
Patna
33
Calcutta
33
Dhaka
34

6. THE POLLUTED RIVER
36
India's drain
36
Cleaning up the Ganges
37

7. THE SACRED RIVER
40
The Ganges is born
40
The holy water
41

8. THE YEARS AHEAD
43

GLOSSARY
46

BOOKS TO READ AND FURTHER INFORMATION
47

INDEX
48

1. 'MOTHER GANGES'

'The Ganga, especially, is the river of India, beloved of her people, round which are
intertwined her memories, her hopes and fears, her songs of triumph, her victories and
her defeats. She has been a symbol of India's age-long culture and civilization, ever
changing, ever flowing and yet ever the same Ganga.'
Jawaharlal Nehru, Prime Minister of India (1947 – 64)

The Ganges is unique. Not because of the river's amazing length or width or other unusual features. Other rivers surpass the Ganges on most of these counts. But no other river can match the reverence and affection that is shown to the Ganges by the people of India. These feelings are reflected in the thousand names given to the river. In addition to its proper Indian name, Ganga, other names include *Sughosha* (meaning 'the melodious'), *Bhagya-janani* ('the creator of happiness'), *Jagada-hita* ('the friend of all that lives and moves') and, perhaps the most telling of all, *Ganga mai* (Mother Ganges), the giver of life.

A village in Bangladesh, in the Ganges delta region.

HIMACHAL
PRADESH

Gangotri
Glacier

C H I N A

N

H I M A L A Y A S

T I B E T

Devprayag

Bhagirathi

Alaknanda

Hardwar

New
Delhi

N
E
P
A
L

Kathmandu

Mt Everest

SIKKIM

BHUTAN

ASSAM

Agra

Yamuna

U T T A R
P R A D E S H

Kanpur

Ganges

Allahabad

Ghaghara

Gandak

Varanasi

Patna

Brahmaputra

Farakka
Dam

BANGLADESH

Dhaka

Padma

Son

B I H A R

Hooghly

WEST BENGAL

Bhopal

M A D H Y A   P R A D E S H

Calcutta

Haldia

S U N D A R B A N S

I N D I A

Sagar
Island

Nagpur

O R I S S A

MAHARASHTRA

BAY OF BENGAL

A N D H R A

P R A D E S H

Hyderabad

0		100		200	300	400 km

0	50	100	150	200 miles

Some 300 million people, more than all the population of the USA, live in the Ganges river basin: 200 million live on the northern plains of India and another 100 million in the delta shared with neighbouring Bangladesh. All these people are dependent on the Ganges, if not for their water, then for their food.

The Ganges also enriches the spiritual lives of millions of Hindus, for whom the river is holy because they believe it is the goddess Ganga come to earth. For this reason, the river is thought of as female and is always referred to as 'she' or 'her'. Hindus worship the river like any god or goddess of their religion, Hinduism, and many want their ashes put in the Ganges after death.

Holy and vital for their survival it may be, but this has not stopped people from abusing the river. Today, the poisonous wastes from homes and factories are choking the Ganges, changing a source of fresh water into a sewer – turning the bringer of life into the destroyer of life. Deforestation, too, has blocked the river

with soil washed off the highlands. No wonder that an angry Mother Ganges regularly bursts her banks after the monsoon rains to take revenge on selfish humans who care little for her future.

Even if the people are not worried, the Indian government most certainly is. The government is so concerned about the state of the river that it has set up the Ganges Action Plan to clean it up. Now India can look forward to a revitalized Ganges; a Ganges which it is hoped will also provide huge amounts of electricity, as well as much-needed water for the drier southern regions of India.

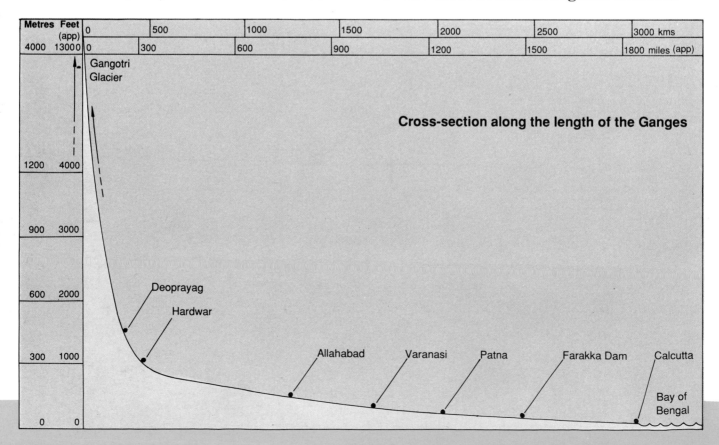

Cross-section along the length of the Ganges

6

2. FROM THE MOUNTAINS TO THE SEA

The upper Ganges

Most people consider the true source of the Ganges to be the meltwaters of the Gangotri glacier, 4,255 m up in the Himalaya Mountains. The powerful little river created by the thawing ice is called the Bhagirathi. Some 200 km downstream, it is joined by the Alaknanda and their combined waters become known as the River Ganges.

At this point, the Ganges is a typical mountain torrent, using the power produced by its steep fall to the plains to carve a narrow channel through the rock, squirming through narrow gorges and thundering over innumerable rapids. After plunging nearly 3,800 m in the first 500 km, the Ganges reaches the plains at Hardwar. From here onwards, it descends to sea level at a slower pace, dropping 300 m in the next 1,900 km

The Bhagirathi (left) and Alaknanda Rivers merge to become the Ganges at the town of Devprayag.

How the Himalayas were formed

India and Asia have not always been joined together. Originally, they were separated by a sea, into which flowed two large rivers, the present-day Indus and Brahmaputra, and many smaller ones. All the sediment brought down by them gradually built up in layers on the seabed.

Then, about 25 million years ago, enormous forces within the earth's crust began pulling India and Asia together. When they collided, all the layers of sediment in the sea were crushed and squeezed upwards, forming the 'fold mountains' known today as the Himalayas (*right*). The Ganges was one of the rivers created after the appearance of the Himalayas.

India and Asia are still being pulled towards each other, not smoothly, but in sudden jerks which can cause earthquakes. Some of the most powerful and destructive earthquakes in the world have occurred among the Himalayas. In October 1991, for example, 1,000 people died in an earthquake which devasted Uttarkashi, just north of Hardwar.

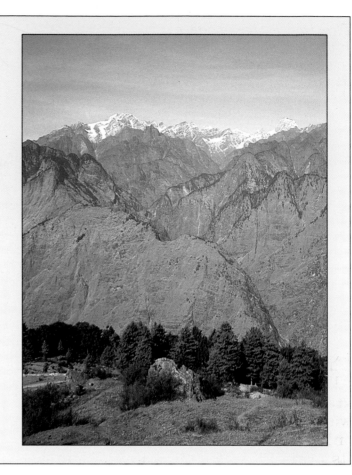

to its delta in the Bay of Bengal.

The Ganges has helped to develop these plains, not merely by depositing another layer of topsoil when it floods its banks every summer, but also by providing the land with water for irrigation. Nowhere is this vital role more noticeable that at Hardwar, where much of the water is diverted by a dam into the Upper Ganges Canal, reducing the river to little more than a tributary; the dam also produces hydroelectricity. When it was constructed, in 1854, the canal was the largest irrigation system in the world, supplying 607,500 hectares of farmland. The Ganges only becomes a major river again at Allahabad, where it is joined by the Yamuna.

The Ganges at Hardwar, at the start of its long journey across the plains. The river curves away in the background. In the foreground is the Upper Ganges Canal.

This impressive, modern suspension bridge joins the river's two banks at Rishikesh, in the foothills of the Himalayas.

The middle Ganges

During this stage of its course, from Allahabad to Patna, the Ganges gradually grows in size, swollen by the waters of the Yamuna. But it remains only a medium-sized river the length of its journey through the state of Uttar Pradesh.

Soon after the city of Varanasi, it enters the state of Bihar and takes on the character of a truly major river. Broad and filled with sediment from several large tributaries, including the Ghaghara, Gandak and Son, it meanders sluggishly across the huge flat plain. Here the river is unpredictable in behaviour – dozing for most of the year, then alarmingly destructive; one year washing away farmland, the next, shifting course to provide more land. The Ganges' plain is littered with cities once on the river's banks, but no longer. Rajmahal, on the borders of the states of Bihar and West Bengal, was left high and dry in the early 1860s when the Ganges moved 5 km away. Ten years later, the river was 10 km distant; today, it has returned, but too late: Rajmahal is a ghost town.

How the Ganges' plain was formed
In geological terms, the Himalayas are young, so their rocks are still soft and easily eroded by the monsoon rains: more than 1,000 tonnes of rock are worn away from each square kilometre every year. After the formation of the Himalayas, there was a deep valley between them and the Deccan, as the highlands of southern India are called. Over millions of years, this valley was filled up with all the rocky sediment washed off the mountains, to form a huge flat plain, 320 km wide, over which the Ganges flows to the sea.

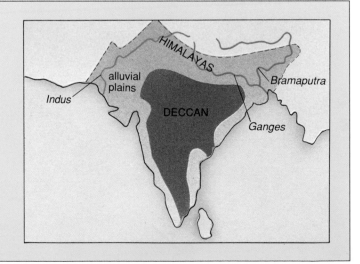

Nowadays, it is hard to imagine that this part of the Ganges was once a busy commercial waterway linking the Bay of Bengal with the central plains. Two hundred years ago the river was navigable all year round, so in 1794 the East India Company began operating a regular paddle-steamer service between Calcutta and Allahabad. Late in the following century, it had to be closed down because the river had become too shallow for the ships: it was difficult even to reach Patna. The Upper Ganges Canal had robbed the river of much of its water and deforestation of the highland areas had filled the Ganges and its tributaries with large amounts of silt.

Right *Hanging out the washing after a day spent ferrying people across the river.*

Below *Pilgrims' boats at the point where the Ganges and Yamuna meet at Allahabad.*

The lower Ganges

Beyond Patna the dry plains of Bihar give way to the wetlands of West Bengal, the final Indian state in the Ganges' journey to the sea. The main river continues on into Bangladesh, where it unites with the Brahmaputra River to become the River Padma before continuing into the Bay of Bengal. Meanwhile, a tributary, confusingly called the Bhagirathi again, heads directly south to join the River Hooghly and they then flow into the Bay of Bengal. This used to be the main exit of the Ganges until the twelfth century, when the land tilted, draining the water out of the Bhagirathi and into the Padma.

Below *There are few roads and no railways in the Sundarbans so boats are the main form of transport.*

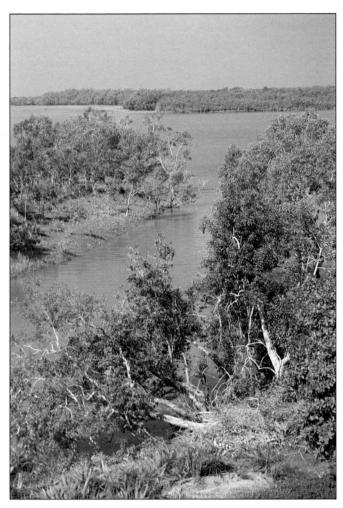

Above *The trees that cover most of the muddy islands in the Sundarbans are often almost submerged by the high levels of water.*

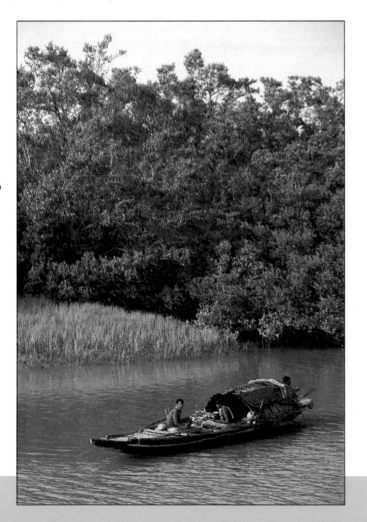

The Hooghly and the Padma Rivers share an enormous delta, 130,000 sq km in size. At its raggedy edge, where the land fans out into the sea, forming over fifty muddy islands separated by a maze of channels, there is the world's largest estuarine (river mouth) forest: 26,000 sq km of mangrove trees. This is the Sundarbans, so called because of the sundari trees that once grew here in abundance. The trees have disappeared; cut down for housing and boat-building or killed by the increased salinity of the water, as the delta clogs up with silt.

11

Sagar Island, at the mouth of the Hooghly, is traditionally the place where the Ganges ends its journey, emptying into the Bay of Bengal with such force that its sludgy waters can be seen 600 km out in the ocean.

Opposite *Villagers wash in one of the many channels of the Ganges delta.*

Wildlife in the Ganges' basin

The Ganges' plains were once covered in dense forests, full of wild animals. As these were cut down, the animals retreated to the highland forests. Even here the tiger, elephant and musk deer have not been safe from hunters after their skins, their tusks for ivory or, in the case of musk deer, the scent glands used in perfumes. Animal numbers have declined so much that special conservation parks have been opened where they can live in safety.

Other animals living in the forests include bears, leopards, foxes, jackals, boars and monkeys, as well as snakes and monitor lizards. In the air, you can see over 500 species of birds, from parakeets and kingfishers to storks and woodpeckers.

There are many varieties of fish in the Ganges' waters, including salmon and trout. The river is famous for crocodiles (*see below*) and the closely related gharial, with its distinctive long, thin snout. The gharial eats only fish, whereas the crocodile will also go for human and animal flesh.

In the Sundarbans the Royal Bengal tiger is equally at home on land as in water.

The Sundarbans

The Sundarbans is a unique environment where plants and animals are continuously adapting to a habitat that has a daily cycle of high and low tides, bringing in and then flushing out large quantities of nutrients. Eighty per cent of the land is under water at high tide. The Sundarbans is situated at the meeting-point of sea and river water and the slightest change in the flow alters the salinity of the water. This affects plants and, later on, the animals that feed on them.

The tiger is an interesting example of how a species has been forced to adapt to an ever-changing environment. Here, a tiger is equally at home on dry land and in the water. It is capable of swimming up to 10 km between islands in search of prey. It is not fussy whether it dines on seafood – fish, crab or turtle – or on a land-based deer, monitor lizard, wild boar or even the occasional human. Of the 300 Royal Bengal tigers remaining in the Sundarbans, about 60 are man-eaters; in 1991 they killed 32 people.

The trees, too, which spend half their lives almost afloat, have developed long, drooping root systems to anchor themselves in the ground. Some even have roots which poke up through the mud at low tide to take in air.

3. WEATHER AND CLIMATE

The three seasons

There are three distinct seasons in northern India and Bangladesh. The winter months, from November to February, are mild and dry: daytime temperatures do not go above 25°C and the rainfall is less than 20 mm a month. Spring, from March to May, is very hot and dry: the rainfall remains low, but temperatures soar to 40°C. The summer months, from June to October, are hot and very wet: temperatures drop a little and the rainfall becomes very heavy. In July over 400 mm of rain falls in the foothills of the Himalayas and the delta, and 300 mm on the plains in between.

Each year, during the monsoon season, huge areas of Bangladesh are flooded.

The monsoon

The rain is brought by the winds, called the monsoon, which sweep across the Indian Ocean from the south-west, reaching the tip of India at the end of May. The increase in temperatures during the spring heats up the land more quickly than the water in the surrounding sea. As the land gets warmer, so the air above it becomes hotter and rises, causing a decrease in the air pressure. Out to sea, the pressure remains higher above the cooler water. By the end of May, the difference in pressure between the two is so great that air is literally sucked inland. As the winds are dragged over the ocean, they pick up moisture which is dropped as rain on the parched land.

15

The monsoon winds which pass to the south of India bend left and head up the east coast towards Calcutta, where they split into two streams. The right-hand stream of the monsoon branches off north-eastwards, to drop its rain on Bangladesh. The left one turns up the valley of the Ganges. The further west it travels, the drier it becomes, so that farmers on the plains of the upper Ganges receive much less rain than those in West Bengal. West Bengal and Bangladesh are the wettest areas; the central regions of the states of Bihar and

Some monsoon facts

The following information shows how the monsoon affects the lives of the people of India and Bangladesh.

- The monsoon brings 80 per cent of Bangladesh's yearly rainfall.
- Nearly 60 per cent of Bangladesh's rice is grown during the monsoon season.
- Most of Bangladesh is flat and very low, no more than 4.5 m above sea level. In a good year, only 20 per cent of the land is flooded during the monsoon; in a bad year, 80 per cent is flooded.
- The Ganges, reduced to just a trickle in many parts during the dry winter months, comes alive after the monsoon, often with terrible consequences. In 1982, in Uttar Pradesh state, 15,000 houses were destroyed and 2,000 villages cut off, as, swollen by the rains, the Ganges eroded its banks and shifted its course, flooding nearby land.
- If the monsoon fails (as it last did in 1987) and only a little rain comes, it has been estimated that 15 million Indians are put out of work, because their jobs rely on agriculture.
- In the summer of 1877, 5 million Indians starved to death when the monsoon rains did not arrive; a century earlier, 10 million perished in a famine in Bengal.
- Indian meteorologists report that monsoon failures have become more frequent in the last twenty years: 1987 was the ninth year in a decade when the monsoon failed to bring rain to northern India. Fortunately, India is better able today to deal with a drought: weather satellites provide advance warning so that wells can be dug and plans made to distribute food.

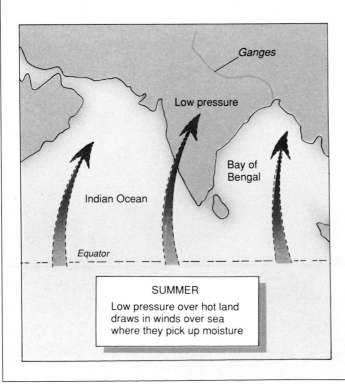

SUMMER
Low pressure over hot land draws in winds over sea where they pick up moisture

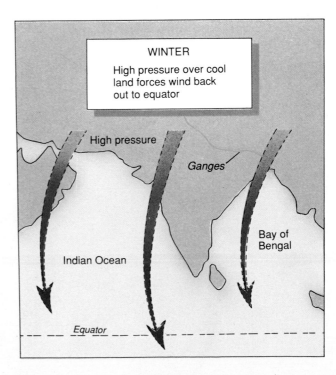

WINTER
High pressure over cool land forces wind back out to equator

Uttar Pradesh are the driest. In some years, there is so little rain here that there have been droughts and terrible famines and millions of people have died.

People cannot rely on the amount of rain the monsoon will bring. In some years, it is only small and farmers' crops can be ruined. In other years, it can be too much and villages and cities are flooded with deep water.

Fierce storms at the end of the summer are powerful enough to lift huge ships out of the river. This one has been stranded near Dhaka.

Raised banks protect villages in the Sundarbans from high water levels in the delta's channels.

Cyclones and surges

At the end of September, as the temperature drops and the land cools, the air pressure above it rises, forcing the monsoon winds back out to sea. As they retreat southwards to the equator, fierce storms, called cyclones, are stirred up over the Bay of Bengal and lash the coasts of Bangladesh and east India. Strong winds funnel the sea into the shallow, narrow channels of the Ganges' delta, creating a huge surge of water, frequently more than 4 m high and topped with waves equally tall. This massive wall of water tumbles over the

Mobarak Ullah Mazumder

'I am the captain of the paddle-steamer *Ghazi* which travels from Dhaka to Khulna and back again, along the waterways of the Ganges' delta in Bangladesh. The 650-km round trip can only be done during the dry season, when the channel markers and river banks can be clearly seen. It is too risky in the wet summer months, because the water rises so high that most of the markers and banks are hidden. Even though we carry a pilot who knows the channels, the *Ghazi* often runs aground.'

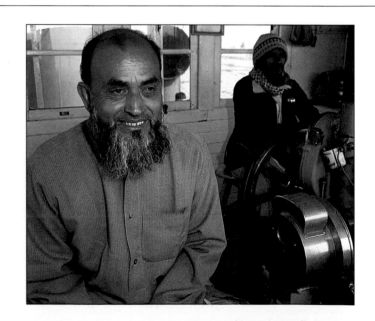

The effects of global warming on Bangladesh

If scientists are correct about global warming there could be a catastrophe in Bangladesh. Most of the country is so low-lying that even a small rise in the level of the oceans could have devastating consequences, drowning many people and flooding thousands of hectares of land. Weather scientists are also worried that global warming will increase the power of cyclones, making them even more destructive in years to come.

These houses in Bangladesh are built on stilts to protect them from floods.

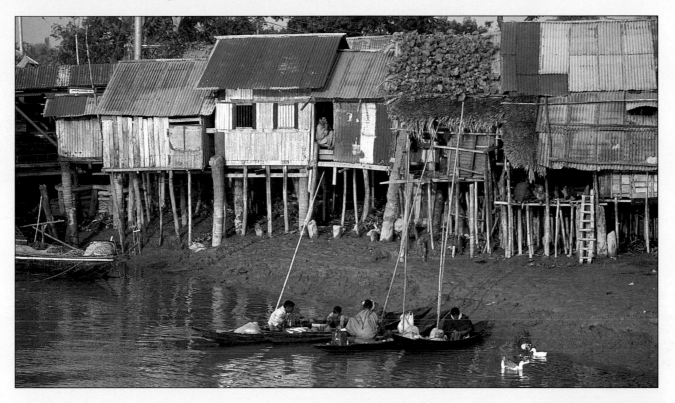

low, unprotected islands of the delta, destroying and sweeping away everything in its path. A particularly bad cyclone devastated Bangladesh in November 1970, when winds of over 200 kph and an 8-metre high surge killed 300,000 people, left one million homeless, drowned half a million cattle, and washed away most of the rice crop and the country's fishing boats.

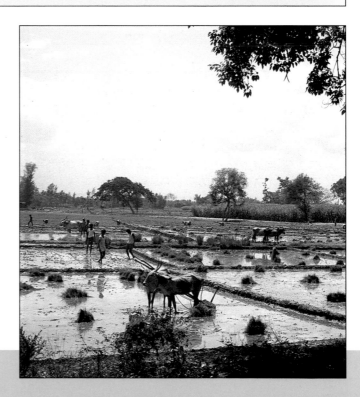

Rice paddy fields in the low-lying lands of the delta are often flooded during the monsoon season.

4. AGRICULTURE

The effects of weather and terrain

Subsistence farming is the main type of agriculture on the Ganges' plains and delta. This means that the farmers are able to cultivate enough food for their own needs, to feed their families, but not enough to sell for an income.

Rainfall is the biggest problem for farmers; not just how much, but when it falls. Little rain falls during the winter months from November to May; most comes in the summer, brought by the monsoon.

In the highland areas, where there is snow and ice in winter, both farmers and their crops are affected by the freezing temperatures. Down on the plains, the very hot summer temperatures mean that farmers have to do all their work early in the mornings and evenings, resting at home in the blisteringly hot afternoons.

The plains and the delta are very flat, so they are easily farmed, with bullocks being used to plough the soil. The steep-sided valleys of the mountains and foothills are much more difficult and

Terraced farmland on the steep slopes of the Alaknanda valley in the Himalayas.

there all the work has to be done by hand. The land has to be terraced to prevent the soil from being washed away by the rain. But although the soil is thin and stony, a wide variety of crops are cultivated, including fruits (apples, oranges and lemons), wheat, vegetables (tomatoes, cauliflowers and cabbages) and even some tea. On the lowlands, the deep, rich alluvium, washed down by the rivers, is ideal for growing crops.

Fertile soil
The sediment brought down from the mountains by the Ganges is ground down to fine particles on its journey to the plain, and mixed up with mud and sand to form alluvium. This is a fertile soil, full of the nutrients plants thrive on, so it is ideal for farming. A new layer of alluvium is brought down from the highlands every year after the snow melts and the monsoon arrives. When rivers flood or alter course, this is spread over new areas.

Right *Few farmers in India can afford modern machines to help them in their work.*

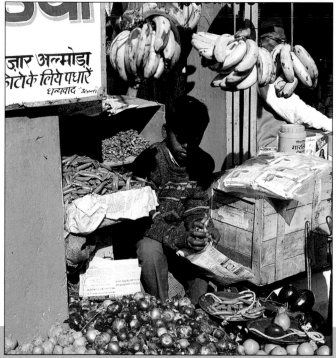

Left *Locally grown fruit and vegetables on sale at a shop in a mountain village in the valley of the Alaknanda.*

21

The crops

Little rain for much of the year means that farmers need to grow two types of crops to get the maximum use from their land: a winter crop that needs only a little rain and a summer one that needs a lot of rain.

These crops are called *rabi* and *kharif*. *Rabi* crops require lower temperatures and rainfall than *kharif* crops, so they are sown at the end of the rainy season, in October and November. They are harvested in April and May, before the start of the monsoon. *Rabi* crops include wheat, barley and gram (seed plants similar to beans).

Kharif crops need heat and moisture, so they are planted just before the monsoon and harvested when it finishes, in October and November. *Kharif* crops include rice, maize, millets, cotton and sugar-cane.

In the delta region, the farmers can grow only one crop a year, a *kharif* crop which is either rice or jute: both need heavy rain during their growing season. In the dry winter months, the river level is low, so tides penetrate further upstream in the delta, increasing the water's salinity and making it harmful to use on crops. The farmers lack the pumps needed to draw fresh water from deep under ground to irrigate the land. As they are unable to farm, they turn to fishing, gathering honey or wood-cutting.

Many people earn a living from the rich supplies of fish in the Ganges delta.

Left *The sandy silt of the river bed near Kanpur is good for growing fruit and vegetables in the winter. During the monsoon, all this land is flooded as the rains swell the river.*

Right *One of the dams at Hardwar at the beginning of the Upper Ganges Canal. The canal is used to irrigate land which would otherwise be difficult to farm.*

Irrigation

A long dry season means that a farmer must irrigate his fields to prevent the *rabi* harvest being ruined. In the driest areas of the Ganges' plains, canals provide the main form of irrigation. At Hardwar, for instance, a dam diverts much of the river's water into the Upper Ganges Canal, from where smaller channels distribute water among the farmers' fields. Further downstream, water is supplied by wells. Traditional wells involve using a bucket to draw up water from a deep hole in the ground. Modern wells are tube-wells, where a long plastic tube is sunk into the ground and the water is sucked up by a motor-driven pump, powered either by electricity, petrol or diesel.

The monsoon can bring too much rain in some years and too little in others. Some years the monsoon arrives on time; other years, it is late. So farmers cannot rely on the monsoon and they must be prepared to irrigate their land even in the summer, especially when the monsoon fails.

Social and political problems

In India people have large families, and when parents die, land is divided up equally between all the sons of a family. Over the centuries, this has meant that farms, which once may have been large and profitable, have been broken up into smaller and smaller units as they have been handed down from one generation to the next. Today, many farms can supply only enough food for their owners, but cannot bring in an income.

As a consequence, some farmers decide to buy extra land. With no savings, they are forced to borrow from a local moneylender, usually at a very high rate of interest. Or they may rent extra fields, paying the landowner either in cash or with a part of the harvest. Either way, it is very costly and farmers are faced with a crippling debt which is very often passed on to their sons.

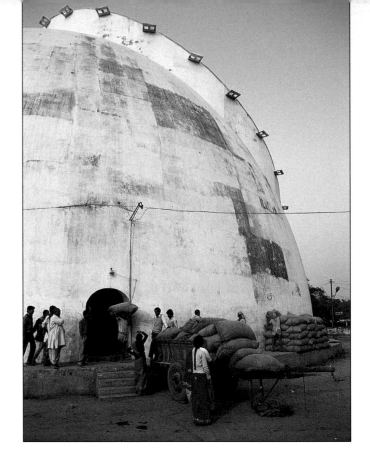

This granary was built in 1786 to store food for use in times of famine.

Jute grown in the delta region is taken by boat for sale in Dhaka.

24

Bullocks are a common sight in rural India. They are used for pulling carts and also to pull ploughs across fields.

The plight of the farmer is made worse by the caste system – a rigid division of Hindus into different social groups. Hinduism is the principal religion of India and higher caste Hindus own most of the land while the lowest caste are often landless labourers.

Political factors cause problems for farmers too. In Western countries, governments have scientists and advisers to help farmers. But in India and Bangladesh, there are few of these and money for agricultural research is limited. In the West, too, cheap bank loans and government grants are available to farmers wanting to expand or invest in new equipment. In India and Bangladesh, such financial help is not so easy to obtain. Without such support, the struggle to modernize defeats many farmers and they are forced to continue with their age-old methods.

All this presents a gloomy picture of farming in India and Bangladesh. In reality, though, the situation has improved a great deal since the 1960s, especially in India. But reforms, while benefiting the wealthier farmers and India as a whole, have also done much damage to the millions of small-scale farmers, who make up the bulk of the agricultural system.

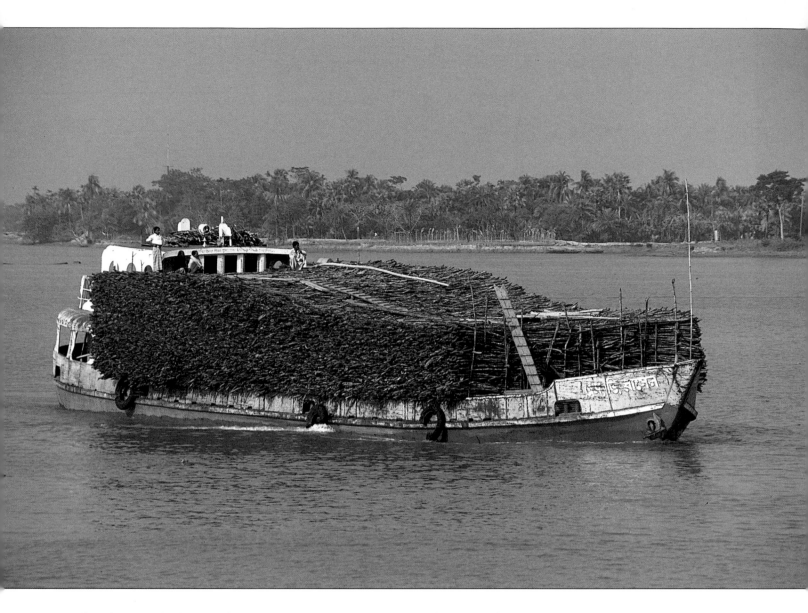

This boat is laden with teak wood for furniture-making. Delta farmers earn a lot of money from growing timber.

The Green Revolution in India

The 'Green Revolution' is the phrase used to describe the replacement of many traditional farming methods in developing countries with up-to-date techniques common in Western nations. In India, the revolution started in the late 1960s, when the government began to introduce major changes.

It was decided that there would be a complete shake-up of the agricultural system in India. Chemical fertilizers were imported, along with new types of strong, disease-resistant seeds which yielded larger harvests than the home-grown varieties. Indian scientists began researching into increasing the production of other crops. Bank loans were provided for tractors, machines, fertilizers and pesticides, and advisers were sent to villages, giving information and advice about improving farming techniques.

While all this was happening, the national transportation system was overhauled to improve the distribution of agricultural supplies and farmers' crops.

The results have been both good and bad. The target of self-sufficiency in food production has almost been reached, and the food shortages, so common in the 1960s, are rarer. Wheat and rice harvests have doubled with the introduction of new varieties of seeds.

And the farmers' standard of living? Here, the reforms have not been so successful. The new seeds need a lot of expensive chemicals and irrigation, which only the wealthier farmers can afford. Poorer farmers have run up debts to buy chemicals and equipment which they find difficulty in paying off. Their quality of life has not improved; indeed, many consider themselves worse off now, especially as they have discovered that some of the new varieties of seeds cannot survive a drought and need extra irrigation, which they cannot afford to provide. Over all, the gap between rich and poor farmers has widened.

The Green Revolution has brought benefits into other parts of the Indian economy. Road and rail networks have been improved, and jobs have been created in the new factories manufacturing agricultural chemicals. But the increased use of chemicals is alarming conservationists and doctors, who are concerned about the damage being done to the environment and to people's health.

The Green Revolution has helped many rich farmers to buy tractors.

5. TRANSPORT, CITIES AND INDUSTRIES

Without water, there can be no life; a nearby source of water has been the priority of all communities throughout history. So it was for the earliest people in northern India, who decided to settle alongside the Ganges because its water had many uses. People used it in their homes for drinking, washing and cooking; for their farm animals and crops; as a source of food; even for recreation.

An important trade route

The first settlers were hunter-gatherers who lived off the animals, fruit and plants in the thick forests which covered the plains. After the discovery of iron tools, making it easier to clear trees for farming land, people switched to growing crops. Cattle were sacred to them, so they were only bred for their milk and to help work the land – something that is still

In Bangladesh it is easier to travel by boat than by either train or bus.

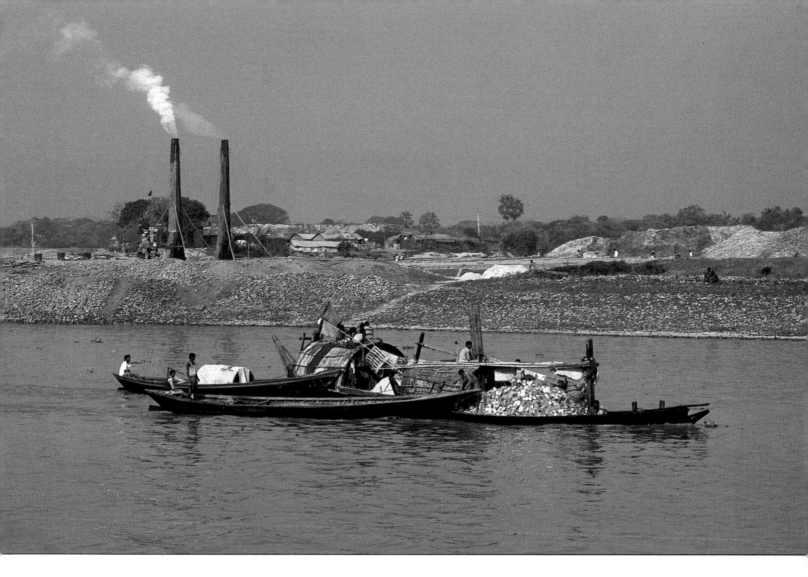

Boats carry cargoes of bricks from a brick-making factory on the river bank near Dhaka.

truc today. The development of agriculture brought about the growth of other occupations and trade. As well as a source of life, the Ganges now became a natural highway along which farmers, craftsmen and merchants travelled, opening up new villages, trades and markets in the forest clearings on its banks. New ideas, too, were spread by these people on their journeys.

Changes in climate, irrigation schemes and deforestation have reduced the water level, so that long stretches of the Ganges are unnavigable. The role of the river as a transporter of goods, people and knowledge has been taken over by roads, railways, aircraft, television and telecommunications. The exception is the delta, where poor road and rail networks mean that boats are still the main means of transport. While the role of the Ganges for transport has declined, the cities on its banks remain important: some because they are historically famous, perhaps once a military base or the capital of a powerful empire; others because of their crafts or industries; and yet others that owe their fame to religion or learning.

Along the upper Ganges, the most important cities are Allahabad and Kanpur; mid-way are Varanasi and Patna; and down near the delta are Calcutta and Dhaka.

Above *One of the few remaining textile mills in Kanpur.*

Opposite *The leather factories in Kanpur are a major source of pollution of the Ganges.*

Allahabad

People have been living here for thousands of years because it is one of the most sacred places in Hinduism. The city is at the meeting point of two holy rivers, the Ganges and the Yamuna, as well as the mythical Saraswati river, which is said to surface here after flowing underground from the Himalayas. The place where the rivers all join, called *sangam,* is very holy to Hindus, and thousands of pilgrims bathe here every year to wash away their sins.

Allahabad was given its present name by the great Mogul emperor Akbar, in 1584. He was a Muslim and he named the city in honour of Allah (God). *Bad* means city, so Allahabad means City of God.

Kanpur

This industrial city of two million people is sometimes called the 'Manchester of India' because of its huge textile mills. The mills are still working, but the cost of modernizing the outdated machinery is causing doubts about their future. More important now is the leather industry, which turns buffalo and cow hides into clothes and shoes for export abroad: it is one of India's major money-earners. The leather industry is also the main polluter of the Ganges, discharging huge amounts of poisonous chemicals into it every day. Another important industry in Kanpur is the manufacture of guns and equipment for the Indian army, a reminder of the time when Kanpur was a British military base.

Varanasi

Varanasi has been a centre of religion, culture and learning for over 3,000 years. Many Hindus choose this place to have their bodies cremated – they believe it is favoured by the gods – so its two electric crematoria and centuries-old burning ghats (riverside steps), with their blazing pyres of wood, are kept busy: they dispose of 40,000 corpses every year. At nearby Sarnath, the Buddha preached his first sermon on Buddhism, back in the fifth century BC. Today, tourists from all over India and the world visit this city of one million inhabitants, providing employment for many workers in hotels, restaurants and shops. The other main industries are silk weaving, wooden handicrafts and jewellery.

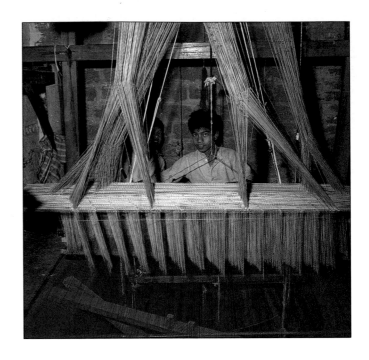

Many of the workers in the silk factories of Varanasi are young children.

A busy street in Calcutta, the largest and most densely populated city in India.

32

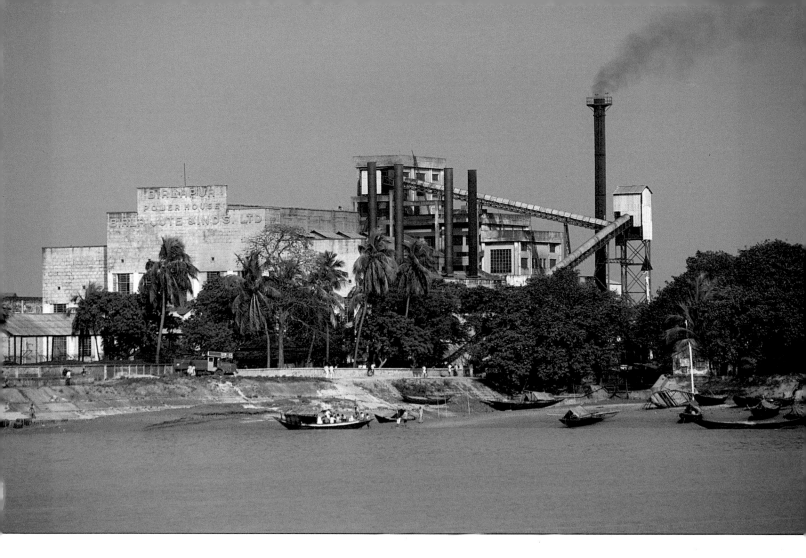

A jute factory in Calcutta. Jute-processing has been important to Calcutta for centuries.

Patna

The remains of Pataliputra, the capital of the ancient Mauryan kingdom, have been excavated near Patna. From here, between 268 and 231 BC, the emperor Ashoka ruled a powerful empire. Patna is less influential today and its territory is much smaller: it is the capital of the state of Bihar, one of the poorest in India, and famous for the long-grained rice grown in great quantities around it. In 1660, the tenth and last *guru* (leader) of the Sikh religion, Govind Singh, was born here. The temple, or *gurudwara,* built in his honour is one of the holiest Sikh shrines and visited by many pilgrims.

Calcutta

With a population of 12 million, Calcutta is the largest city in India (and one of the largest in the world). Strictly speaking, Calcutta is not on the Ganges, but on the River Hooghly. It was the headquarters of the East India Company and became the capital of all the British territories in India until 1911, when the centre of power was moved to New Delhi.

The city was greatly affected by the partition of India after independence from Britain in 1947: the jute farms, on which its factories and port had thrived, now belonged to East Pakistan (the former name of Bangladesh); and millions of Hindu refugees poured over the border, fleeing from persecution in a country created specifically for Muslims.

Since then, new jute farms have been opened to supply the sixty factories in Calcutta. Although the jute industry is still a major employer, engineering has become more important in recent years. The Hooghly silts up easily, which has prevented the development of the port for large sea-going ships, so a new port is being built downstream at Haldia, next to a large petrol refinery.

War between India and Pakistan, and between East and West Pakistan, have added to the refugee problem; a problem made worse by people arriving from the countryside seeking a better life in the city. It has been estimated that *at least* 100,000 people live and sleep on Calcutta's streets. In addition, 4 million people live in cramped, one-roomed homes, often flooded by the monsoon rains.

Dhaka

Once the chief city of the Indian state of East Bengal, Dhaka became the capital of East Pakistan when Pakistan was created after Indian independence. Unhappy with the way it was treated by West Pakistan, the East broke away in 1971 to become Bangladesh. Today, the country's defencelessness in the face of natural disasters, caused by its position near the mouths of the Ganges and Brahmaputra Rivers, and its enormous population, make Dhaka the capital of one of the poorest nations in the world. Bangladesh is heavily dependent on agriculture, with few industries, most of which are concentrated around Dhaka. The main industries are the manufacture of cement, bricks and steel.

Right *A crowded pavement in the heart of Dhaka, the capital of Bangladesh.*

The East India Company
This was a trading company formed in 1600 by the British government to take part in the spice trade in the East Indies in Southeast Asia. After being driven out of the islands by Dutch colonists, the company developed trade with India. The East India Company became involved in politics, acting for the British government from the eighteenth to mid-nineteenth century. Following a revolt of the Indian troops in 1857, sometimes known as the Indian Mutiny, power was transferred from the East India Company to the British government, and the Company ceased to exist in 1874.

The Writers Building in Calcutta (*below*) was once the head office of the East India Company.

6. THE POLLUTED RIVER

India's drain

For most of history, people all over the world have abused rivers, taking the fresh water and replacing it with their own waste. Regrettably, the Indians' treatment of the Ganges is no exception to this behaviour.

Over the centuries, as cities and industries developed along its banks, so the river became steadily more filthy. Recent surveys estimate that 1,000 million litres of waste liquids are discharged every day into the Ganges – much of it untreated, raw sewage and harmful industrial chemicals. Warnings about the consequences were ignored until the early 1980s, by which time the Ganges resembled an enormous drain. Where once the river's waters had been a source of life, they now carried bacteria and poisons capable of causing death.

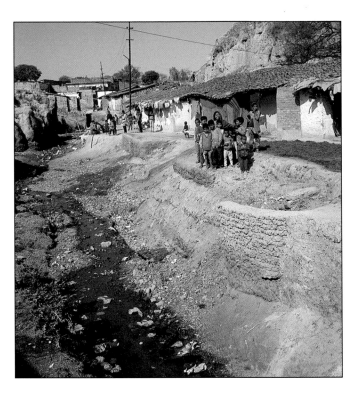

Untreated domestic and industrial waste flows from this village into the Ganges.

As part of the Ganges Action Plan, the Netherlands government is helping to build waste-treatment plants in Kanpur to reduce the amount of chemicals being discharged into the Ganges.

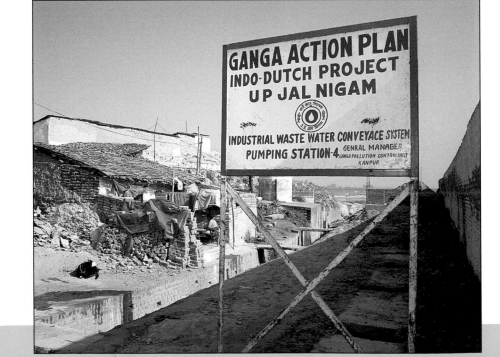

Cleaning up the Ganges

A massive clean-up programme, the Ganges Action Plan (GAP), was started by the Indian Government in 1985. It had two aims.

Firstly, there needed to be a considerable reduction in the amount of untreated waste pouring into the river from factories and homes.

Secondly, with the help of widespread publicity, the GAP was to make everybody aware of the dangers of pollution so that they would have more respect for the environment and for the river.

To achieve the first aim, the government has turned to Western countries, particularly Britain and the Netherlands, for assistance. Together, they are building water-treatment plants to purify liquid waste before it is dumped in the river. One problem is that few Indian homes have lavatories, nor are there many public ones for the people to use. Instead they make use of the banks of the Ganges. The government cannot afford to provide lavatories in every home but more public toilets are being built, and sewage systems are being improved so that the amount of raw waste flowing directly into the river is far less than it was.

Another issue being tackled is a sensitive religious one, for the GAP has been challenging some of the centuries-old funeral customs of Hinduism. After death, devout Hindus want to be cremated on the banks of the Ganges and their ashes scattered over the water.

This treatment plant at Varanasi prevents raw sewage draining into the river.

Traditional Hindu funeral pyres on the river bank at Patna.

If the corpses are burnt properly, this is no problem, but many people cannot afford to buy enough wood for a funeral pyre, so half-burnt bodies end up in the river. Very poor people often throw their relatives' bodies straight into the water. Furthermore, according to Hindu customs, the corpses of children under eleven years old, priests, and adults who have died from certain diseases, are also placed directly in the river. The result of all these practices is that a decaying body in the Ganges is an everyday sight. The government is encouraging people to use the electric crematoria that have been built in cities like Varanasi and Calcutta, but although these are cheaper than a traditional wood pyre,

Rajiv Kapur

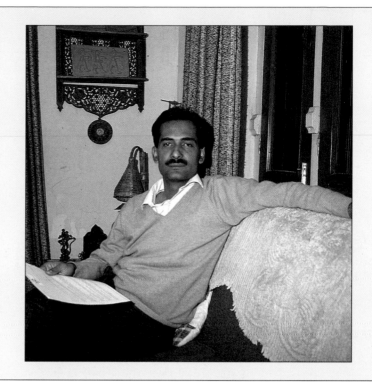

'I started the pressure group, Environment India, to draw attention to pollution in Kanpur and in the River Ganges. In Kanpur the leather tanneries dump thousands of litres of poisonous chemicals into the river every day. But the leather industry provides jobs for 65,000 workers and also earns a lot of money. So no one wants to upset the factory owners by demanding the installation of expensive treatment plants. We can't go on like this forever, otherwise there will be nothing left for our grandchildren. Environment India is opening people's eyes and minds, so there is hope for a better tomorrow.'

people are reluctant to change their ways, even though this will help clean up the river and save trees.

Work is now in progress in twenty-seven Indian towns and cities all along the length of the river. The quality of the water is regularly checked by taking samples of it for testing in laboratories. Already these have shown noticeable improvements in the river's cleanliness.

People, too, with the help of exhibitions, discussions and competitions, are now more aware of the issues involved and how they can help to improve the situation.

Poisonous factory waste clogs up the Ganges near Kanpur.

7. THE SACRED RIVER

The Ganges is born

The religion of most people in India is Hinduism. One of its many myths concerns the creation of the Ganges. Far back in time, northern India was ruled by King Sagar, proud father of 60,000 sons! These youths, so the story goes, were so disrespectful to Kapil Muni, a seaside holy man, that he reduced them to ashes with a withering look.

When the distraught king turned to the gods for help, they replied that his sons would be brought back to life only if their sinful remains were cleansed by the waters of the goddess Ganga, a river then residing in the heavens. After much praying and pleading by another holy man, Bhagirath, Ganga reluctantly consented to descend to earth. To break her fall, the god Shiva stepped in the way and let the river tumble gently through his long hair on to the Himalayas. Ganga then flowed across India to the edge of the ocean, where she washed over the ashes and restored King Sagar's sons to life – an event commemorated every January with a festival on Sagar Island, at the mouth of the Hooghly River. This ceremony is attended by hundreds of thousands of Hindu pilgrims from all over India.

Journey's end; pilgrims bathing during the annual festival on Sagar Island, at the point where the Ganges enters the Bay of Bengal.

The holy water

This mythical story explains why Hindus have always respected the river – a river often described by them as *Parabrahma-svarupini:* the 'Embodiment of the Supreme Spirit', who is called Brahma, the creator of the universe. The Ganges represents one of the many gods and goddesses of Hinduism. In the same way that they pray to a statue of a god in a temple, so Hindus pray to the river, asking the goddess Ganga for her blessing and her forgiveness. If they live alongside the river, their worship will involve bathing in it twice a day, at dawn and dusk, and offering the river gifts of flowers and food. If their home is far away, devout Hindus will make a special effort to attend a festival at one of the many sacred places on the river.

Pilgrims from all over India come to the Ganges to collect and take home some of its holy water.

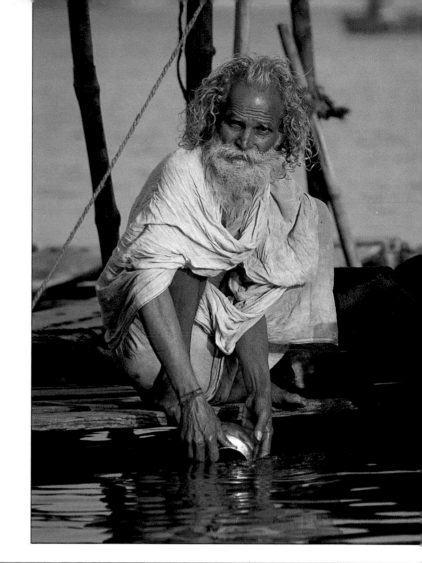

Bolegiri

'I am a *sadhu,* which means holy man. A *sadhu* chooses to spend his life thinking about god and religion instead of having a job, home and family. In India, people don't think this is unusual, so there are many *sadhus.* Like me, most of them wear orange-coloured clothes, the sacred colour of Hinduism. The markings on my forehead show that I am a follower of the god Shiva. I spend my life visiting all the sacred places on the Ganges, as well as the other shrines in India dedicated to Shiva. Besides a blanket and a small bag, I have no possessions. I eat and sleep in temples and hostels and people pay for my rail and bus tickets.'

Afterwards, they will take home a container of its water to use in religious ceremonies.

Whatever distance they travel or however they keep it, the water will always remain fresh. This is one of the peculiar properties of the Ganges that has never been satisfactorily explained: something in the water kills off harmful bacteria, so that it is free of the germs that turn it stale and spread diseases. However, in recent years, the water has become so polluted that scientists doubt whether the Ganges is capable of keeping itself pure, and have started the campaign to clean it up which is discussed in the previous chapter. But no matter how filthy it appears to Western eyes, millions of Hindus continue to bathe in it, convinced that their river goddess will do them no harm and will, in fact, bring them good luck and a long and healthy life.

The Ganges is good for you – fact or faith?

Like most of the world's rivers, just looking at the Ganges is enough to put you off swimming in it or drinking its water. Yet thousands of Indians do this everyday and survive, even downstream of the poisonous pollution from Kanpur's leather factories. Do they build up a resistance or is there really something in the water that keeps it germ-free?

Some scientists say that medicinal herbs in the mountains are responsible for it. Geologists maintain it is the radioactive minerals in the rocky sediment from the Himalayas. Whatever the reason, the Ganges' ability to clean itself is a fact. However, even if the river can rid itself of harmful bacteria, it is extremely unlikely that it can cancel out life-threatening chemicals so that they are safe to drink. It is the rapid increase in the levels of these poisons in the river that has forced the government to take steps to control the waste that is dumped in the Ganges.

The evening Aarti *ceremony at Hardwar in honour of the goddess Ganga.*

8. THE YEARS AHEAD

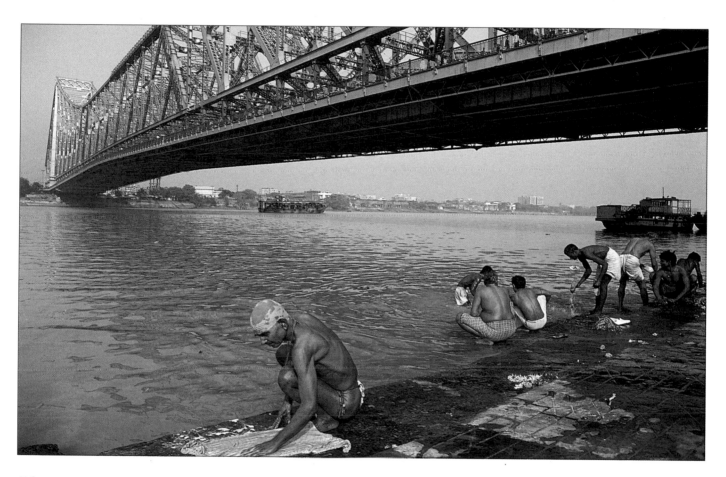

More water now flows under Calcutta's Howrah Bridge, as a result of the building of the Farakka Dam.

Now 25 million years old – even older according to Hindu mythology – the Ganges has had a turbulent history. The river has witnessed the rise and fall of powerful empires; the spread of religions, ideas and trade; the destruction of forests and their replacement with cities and factories which have choked its waters with their waste products; and the devastating impact of the weather on people along its banks.

But, what of the future? Can the people of the Ganges' basin look forward to better times? It would be very difficult to reassure these people, especially as it is already too late to restore the damage which was begun years ago. The most serious of these is the deforestation in Nepal, on India's northern border. Even if this were stopped right now, it would take years to put right. The damage has been done, and Bangladesh, the country most affected, could do nothing to stop it.

The consequences of deforestation

In the early 1940s, 60 per cent of Nepal was covered in forest. There was enough land to grow crops for food for the 5 million people who lived there and trees were replaced at the same rate as they were chopped down for firewood. By the 1980s, the population had grown to 20 million, increasing the demand for wood and farmland so much that only 30 per cent of Nepal remained forest. Now, 500 sq km of trees are being destroyed every year, less than 80 sq km of which are replanted.

Without a protective covering of vegetation to lessen the impact of the monsoon, nor roots to hold the soil, the rains sweep huge quantities of hillside soil into rivers. The Ganges and the Brahmaputra together carry two billion tonnes of sediment to the sea, more than any other river system in the world. The sediment blocks up rivers, reducing their flow and making them more likely to flood. At the delta there is less fresh water flowing out to meet the salty sea water brought in by the tides, and force it back out to sea. This salty water is creeping further up the channels and ruining good farming land. The photograph (*below*) shows the affects of deforestation in Nepal.

Bangladesh, too, has been harmed by a decision of the Indian Government. The Farakka Dam, just inside the Indian border, was built to increase the flow of water in the River Hooghly during the dry winter months, to prevent the port of Calcutta silting up. Inevitably, the dam has altered the amount of water going into Bangladesh.

Now the country's rivers are clogging up faster than ever with sediment and the farmers of Bangladesh have less water for irrigation, at a time when they most need it. Both countries have been in dispute for years, with Bangladesh accusing India of keeping back too much water, and India disagreeing.

A satisfactory solution must be found soon, especially as Bangladesh's river system will be disrupted even more if India carries out plans to transfer water from the Ganges and Brahmaputra to rivers in the south, through a network of canals.

Looking even further into the future, India and its neighbouring countries are desperately short of electricity and demand for it is rising all the time. The best way of providing it would be to harness the power of the fast-flowing rivers in the Himalayas, but can all the countries involved – Nepal, China, India and Bangladesh – agree on how it should be done and how the electricity should be shared? Only time will tell.

Left *Constant dredging of the Hooghly, to remove the silt brought down by the river, enables container ships to dock in Calcutta.*

Right *High above the River Alaknanada, this Himalayan holiday resort gets its electricity from the sun.*

GLOSSARY

Alluvium Fertile soil that has been formed from all the material deposited by a river.
Bacteria Tiny living cells which are sometimes harmful.
Buddha A nobleman and religious teacher from northern India who founded the religion of Buddhism.
Caste A social group or class of people in India.
Colonists People who go to another country to settle there.
Crematoria Buildings where dead bodies are cremated, or burned.
Cyclone A fierce storm with high winds and heavy rain.
Decade A period of ten years.
Deforestation The destruction of large areas of trees.
Delta A flat, fan-shaped area where a river splits into many channels at the end of its course.
Drought A long period without rain.
Environment The surroundings in which humans, plants and animals live, which influence their development and behaviour.
Epicentre The point at which tremors from inside the earth reach the surface and cause earthquakes.
Erode To wear away.
Famine A severe shortage of food when many people do not have enough to eat.
Geological Connected to geology, the study of the earth's rocks, soils etc.
Ghat Steps or a landing place on a riverbank.
Global warming The increase in the average temperatures of the earth, caused by the build-up of gases in the atmosphere which slow down the escape of the sun's heat from the earth.
Habitat The natural home of an animal or plant.
Hinduism The main religion in India. Its followers are called Hindus.
Irrigation Supplying land with water through canals, ditches etc.

Jute A plant, the fibres of which are used to make sacks and ropes.
Mangrove A tree with long roots hanging from its trunk, usually found in marshy areas near the sea.
Mauryan kingdom A kingdom ruled by powerful rulers in the third and second centuries BC. During this time a great civilization flowered in India.
Meander To take a winding course.
Meteorologists People who study the weather.
Mogul emperor A ruler of a Muslim empire that covered large parts of India from the sixteenth to eighteenth centuries.
Monsoon Summer winds that bring rain to much of India and Bangladesh. The word is also used to describe the rainy season.
Muslim Someone who follows the teachings of the Prophet Muhammad.
Mythology A collection of myths or stories about heroes or gods of ancient times.
Navigable Able to be used by boats or ships.
Nutrients Food that plants and animals need to help them grow.
Partition of India The division of the Indian sub-continent into India and Pakistan, after India achieved independence from British rule in 1947.
Pesticides Chemicals that kill pests which are harmful to plants.
Pyre A pile of wood for a cremation.
Rapids Sections of a river where the water is churned up by strong currents or rocks.
Refugees People who are forced to leave their homes because of war, disaster or poverty.
River basin The area that is drained by a large river and all its tributaries.
Salinity The amount of salt in water: it is high in sea water and low in river water.
Sediment All the material, such as sand, gravel, stones and earth, that is carried by a river and deposited on its bed, at its delta, or on its banks when it floods.
Self-sufficiency The ability to supply all your own needs.

46

Sikh A follower of Sikhism, a religion founded in India in the sixteenth century.

Silt Very fine mud or clay carried by a river.

Spiritual Concerned with religion.

Subsistence farming When most of the produce is consumed by the farmer and his family, leaving little or nothing to be sold for money.

Terrain An area of land. This word is used to describe what an area is like; for example 'rocky terrain'.

Tributaries Small rivers that flow into a larger one.

Vulnerable To be exposed to danger.

BOOKS TO READ AND FURTHER INFORMATION

To find out more about the issues discussed in this book, try to get some of these books from your library.

Countries of the World: India by David Cumming (Wayland, 1989)
Flood: by Julia Waterlow (Wayland, 1992)
Focus on India by Shahrukh Husain (Hamish Hamilton, 1986)
Hinduism by Hemant Kanitar (Wayland, 1985)
The Ganges by Gina Douglas (Wayland, 1984)
The Hindu World by Patricia Bahree (Macdonald, 1982)
The Indian Ocean by Pat Hargreaves (Wayland, 1981)
The Partition of India by Hemant Kanitar (Wayland, 1987)

Two photograph books worth looking at are:

A Journey Down the Ganges by Mukul & Saith Kesavan (Lustre Press, 1989)
The Ganges by Raghubir Singh (Thames & Hudson, 1992)

More advanced readers will find the following books interesting:

A Walk Along the Ganges by Berwick Dennison (Century, 1986)
Chasing the Monsoon by Alexander Frater (Penguin, 1991)
Seven Sacred Rivers by Bill Aitken (Penguin, 1992)
Slowly Down the Ganges by Eric Newby (Picador, 1976)

Addresses
Indian Tourist Office
7 Cork Street
London W1X 2AB

For first-hand knowledge about cleaning up the Ganges you could write to:
Environment India,
18 M.I.G. Rattan Lal Nagar, Kanpur.

Picture acknowledgements
All photographs including the cover are by David Cumming except the following: Bruce Coleman/Gerald Cubitt 10 (top),/Erwin and Peggy Bauer 14, /J. Zwaenepoel 25, /John Murray 44; Hutchison Library 15, /S. Dent 19 (lower); Wayland Picture Library/Jimmy Holmes 21 (top), 27. The map on page 5 is by Peter Bull Design. Artwork on pages 6, 9 and 16 is by John Yates.

The author would like to thank Sandeep Chadda and the staff of *The Pioneer* newspaper in Kanpur and Tribhuvan Singh Chauhan for their help.